02069

What are....?

RIVERS

**Andy Owen
and
Miranda Ashwell**

Heinemann
LIBRARY

First published in Great Britain by Heinemann Library
Halley Court, Jordan Hill, Oxford OX2 8EJ
a division of Reed Educational and Professional Publishing Ltd.
Heinemann is a registered trademark of Reed Educational and Professional Publishing Ltd.

OXFORD FLORENCE PRAGUE MADRID ATHENS
MELBOURNE AUCKLAND KUALA LUMPUR SINGAPORE TOKYO
IBADAN NAIROBI KAMPALA JOHANNESBURG GABORONE
PORTSMOUTH NH (USA) CHICAGO MEXICO CITY SAO PAULO

Designed by Susan Clarke
Illustrations by Oxford Illustrators (maps pp.23, 25, 27)
Printed in Hong Kong

02 01 00 99 98
10 9 8 7 6 5 4 3 2 1

ISBN 0 431 02357 3

British Library Cataloguing in Publication Data

Owen, Andy
  What are rivers?. – (Heinemann first library)
  1. Rivers – Juvenile literature
  1. Title II. Ashwell, Miranda III. Rivers
  551.4'83

Acknowledgements
The Publishers would like to thank the following for permission to reproduce photographs:
Aerofilms, p.14; Air Fotos Ltd, p.15; Andy Owen, pp.7, 9; Colourific/Thomas Muscionico, p.12;
Environmental Images/Graham Burns, p.19; Images Colour Library, p.10; Magnum/S.T. Franklin,
p.13; NRSC, pp. 22, 24, 26; Oxford Scientific Films, p.17 (Paul McCullagh), p.20 (Edward
Parker); Panos Pictures/Neil Cooper, p.28; Planet Earth/Adam Jones, p.21; Still Pictures, p.29
(Andre Bartschi), p.16 (Helour Netocny), p.8 (Jim Wark); Telegraph Colour Library/Terry
McCormick, p.11; Tony Stone, p.5, p.18 (Mark Lewis); Wildlife Matters, pp. 4, 6

Cover photograph: Robert Harding Picture Library / Nigel Francis

Our thanks to Betty Root for her comments in the preparation of this book.

Contents

Where rivers begin 4

Mountain rivers 6

Bends in the river 8

Waterfalls 10

Floods 12

Rivers meet the sea 14

Using river water 16

Dirty rivers 18

Work on the river 20

River map 1 22

River map 2 24

River map 3 26

Amazing river facts 28

Glossary 30

More books to read 31

Index 32

Some words are shown in bold, **like this**.
You can find out what they mean by looking
in the Glossary.

Where rivers begin

Rivers begin on high land where it often rains or snows. The start of a river is called the **source**.

This river begins in the mountains where there is a lot of rain and snow

This river begins as
the mountain ice melts

Some rivers start when ice melts. The ice
melts in warm weather. So the river has
most water in spring and summer.

5

Mountain rivers

Streams join to make a river

Water flows down the hill in a stream.
It grows into a bigger river as it is
joined by other streams.

Water tumbles over rocks as it flows down hill. Over many years stones in the stream become round and smooth.

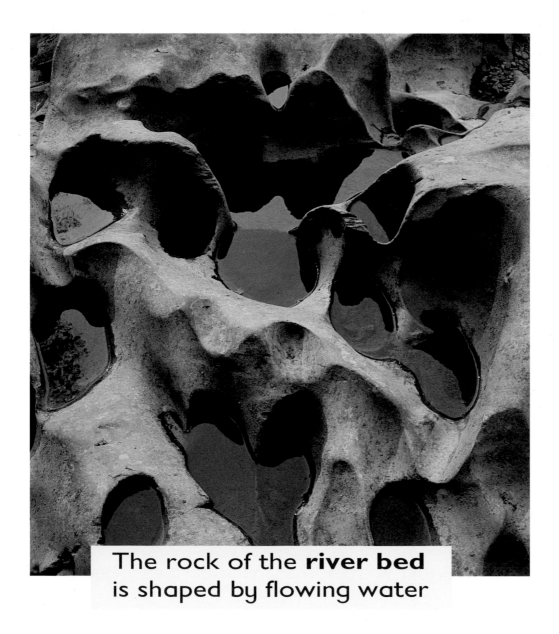

The rock of the **river bed** is shaped by flowing water

Bends in the river

On flat land the river makes large bends.
These bends are called **meanders**.

The flowing water has made these bends

Water flows quickly around the bend.
It wears away the **river bank** and
makes a cliff.

This bank was made by
the meander in the river

Waterfalls

Where a river drops over a steep cliff it makes a waterfall. The rock below is worn away by the falling water.

The falling water makes lots of spray

This raft is thrown about by the wild, white water

The river is wild and rough below the waterfall. The river flows very fast over large rocks. This part of the river is called the **rapids**.

Floods

Heavy rain fills the river. Sometimes water spills over and floods the land. The flat land next to the river is called the **flood plain**.

Some rivers flood every year

Flood water has dropped
mud onto the farmland

When rivers flood they carry mud onto
the land. This mud helps plants grow well.
Flood plains make good farmland.

Rivers meet the sea

By the time the river meets the sea it is very wide. The river flows into the sea. This is called the river **mouth**.

The wide mouth of the river

Large factories have been built on the flat land near the river mouth

The river drops mud at the river mouth. This mud makes flat land next to the river. This land is called **mud flats**.

Using river water

Water is taken from rivers to use on the land. This farmer is lifting water to put on his fields.

Lifting water by hand

This farmer is using a pump to lift water. The pump works very quickly so the farmer has lots of water.

Lifting water with a machine

Dirty rivers

Rubbish from homes and factories gets into the river. It makes the water dirty. This is called **pollution**.

Rubbish makes the water dirty

Fish will live in the river
when it is clean

Dirty water kills fish and river plants.
So people clean the river to make it safe.

Work on the river

People use rivers in many ways.
Fish from the river are sold for food.

This man catches fish with a net

Boats carry people and things along the river. Some rivers are made deep and wide for big ships to use.

This large boat is carrying coal

River map 1

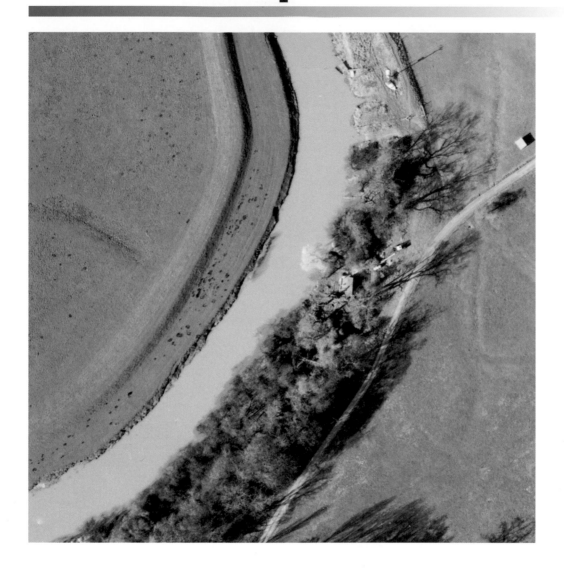

This photo was taken from an aeroplane.
You can see a large bend on a river.
There are fields and a wood next to the river.

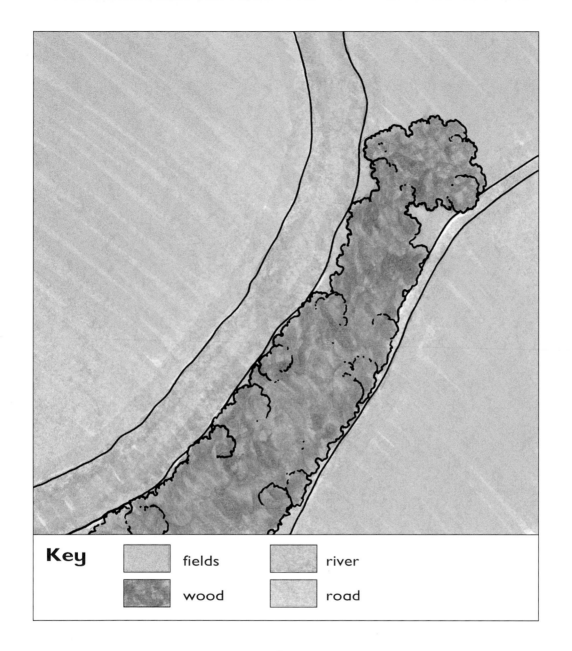

Key

☐	fields	☐	river
☐	wood	☐	road

Maps are pictures of the land.
This map shows us the same place
as the photo.

River map 2

This photo is of the same river. The bend looks smaller but you can see more of the river. You can also see a farm.

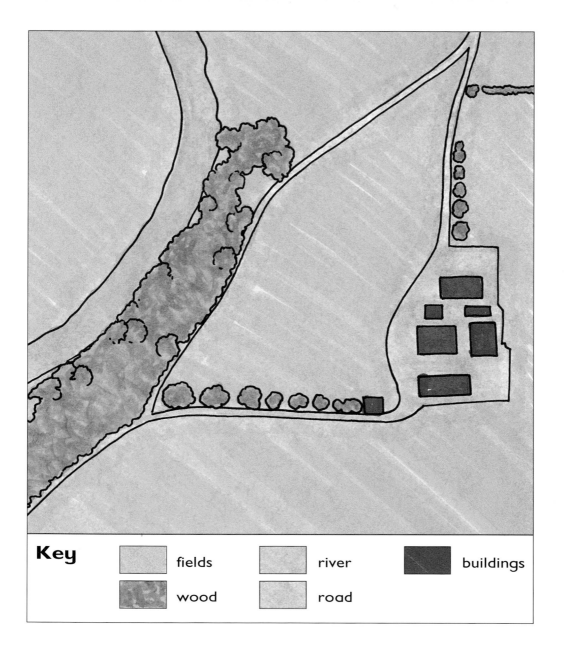

Key

☐	fields	☐	river	▮	buildings
▨	wood	☐	road		

We can understand the map by using the key.
The blue line shows the river and the grey line
shows the road to the farm.

River map 3

In this photo you can see more of the river and more fields. There is a bridge crossing the river at the top of the photo.

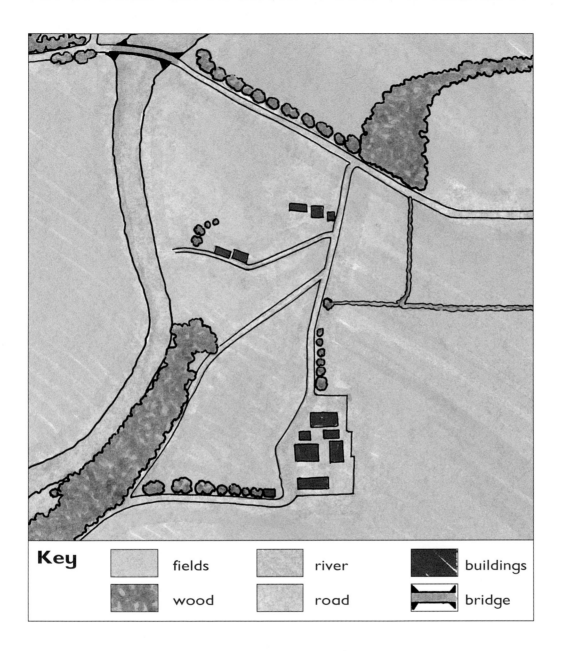

Key

fields	
wood	
river	
road	
buildings	
bridge	

The green on the map shows the fields.
We can see the shape of each field.

Amazing river facts

The River Amazon in South America has more water than any other river in the world. It also flows through the biggest rainforest in the world.

The River Nile is the longest river in the world. It is 7,670 kilometres long. Most of the river flows through a huge desert.

Glossary

flood plain   flat land that is flooded by a river

meanders   bends in a river

mouth   where a river flows into the sea

mud flats   flat land made of mud in or by a river

pollution   dirt and rubbish in the water or air

rapids   where a river flows fast over rocks

river bank   the sides of a river

river bed   the bottom of a river

source   where a stream or river begins

More books to read

Nicole Baxter. *Our wonderful Earth.*
Two-Can, 1997

Claire Llewellyn. *Why do we have? Rivers and Seas.*
Heinemann, 1997

Helena Ramsey. *Step-by-step: Rivers and Lakes.*
Franklin Watts, 1996

Carole Telford and Rod Theodorou.
Amazing Journeys: Down a River.
Heinemann, 1997

Index

flood plain 12, 13

floods 12, 13

maps 23, 25, 27

meanders 8, 9

mouth 14, 15

mud flats 15

pollution 18, 19

rapids 11

river bank 9

river bed 7

river uses 16, 17, 20, 21

source 4

stream 6, 7

waterfalls 10, 11